CW00421491

BEST
OF
BRITISH

A CELEBRATION OF
BRILLIANT BRITAIN

GEORGINA EADE

Michael O'Mara Books Limited

First published in 2008 by
Michael O'Mara Books Limited
9 Lion Yard, Tremadoc Road, London SW4 7NQ

A CIP catalogue record for this book is available from the British Library.

Papers used by Michael O'Mara Books Limited are natural, recyclable
products made from wood grown in sustainable forests. The manufacturing
processes conform to the environmental regulations of the country of origin.

With thanks to Diana Briscoe, Toby Buchan, Kate Gribble,
Stephanie Knox, Anna Marx, Sophie McIvor and Judith Palmer.

Image on page 90: Mary Evans Picture Library

ISBN: 978-1-84317-317-5

1 3 5 7 9 10 8 6 4 2

Designed and typeset by K DESIGN, Somerset.

Printed and bound in Italy by L.E.G.O

www.mombooks.com

CONTENTS

INTRODUCTION

In a remarkable history stretching back thousands of years, Britain has produced countless world-changing inventions and characters. From the ingenuity of the Industrial Revolution to the fortitude of Sir Winston Churchill, British endeavour has impacted far beyond the nation's borders for centuries.

Yet *Best of British* is not a dry-as-dust exercise in listing British accomplishments – after all, we already know that the Beatles, Wimbledon and Marmite (to take just three examples) have secured their places in history.

Instead, this patriotic volume aims to stir national pride and awe readers with a triumphant gallop through a pithy British past, concentrating on the eccentricities that make the nation great, cheering on old favourites –

and revealing little-known facts about modern-day legends.

Shining a light on stand-out military victories, enduring verse, mechanical brilliance, democratic innovation, geographical wonders, iconic British symbols, special dates, the monarchy and those quirks of culture that are British to the core, *Best of British* is a rousing celebration that will have you whipping out a Union Jack flag in no time, joining in a spirited chorus of 'Rule, Britannia!'

THE PROMS

A vibrant symbol of Britain across the globe, these world-famous classical music concerts have delighted millions since their inception.

Origins of the Proms
Robert Newman (1858–1926), manager of the Queen's Hall in London, started the annual concerts in 1895, with Henry Wood (1869–1944) as conductor. Newman's aim was to introduce the public to classical and modern music.

 The two men presented ambitious programmes. Faced with strong anti-German feeling in the wake of the First World War (1914–18), they refused to ban composers such as Wagner, maintaining that 'the greatest examples of Music and Art are world possessions and unassailable even by the prejudices of the hour'.

Sir Henry Wood

The BBC took over the Proms in 1927, which suited its mandate to 'inform, educate and entertain'.

Sir Henry Wood, by then knighted, continued to conduct the orchestra, which became the BBC Symphony Orchestra in 1930.

After Wood's death in 1944, the concerts for a time became known as the Henry Wood Promenade Concerts, although they're now dubbed simply 'the Proms'.

The Royal Albert Hall

In 1941, the Queen's Hall was burned out during the Blitz. The Proms moved to the Royal Albert Hall, where they have remained ever since.

The Royal Albert Hall was the brainchild of Prince Albert (1819–61), consort to Queen Victoria (1819–1901). He sadly died before its grand opening on 29 March 1871; the widowed Queen named it in his memory.

As a 'Prom' means a promenade concert, where part of the audience stands, all the seats on the orchestra and gallery levels of the Albert Hall are specially removed for the event.

The Proms Today
After the Second World War, more orchestras and conductors became involved, and the BBC began to commission new works.

The Proms now include over seventy performances, running from July to September.

The initial vision remains the same: to bring beautiful classical music to the British public.

'It was a sweet view – sweet to the eye and the mind. British verdure, British culture, British comfort, seen under a sun bright, without being oppressive.'

Jane Austen

'Land of Hope and Glory'

Land of Hope and Glory, Mother of the Free,
How shall we extol thee, who are born of thee?
Wider still and wider shall thy bounds be set;
God, who made thee mighty, make thee mightier yet.
God, who made thee mighty, make thee mightier yet.

'Land of Hope and Glory' is a staple – and, for many promenaders, the high point – of the Last Night of the Proms.

First performed at the coronation of Edward VII (1841–1910) in August 1902, the tune is by Sir Edward Elgar (1857–1934), from his *Pomp and Circumstance March No. 1*, with lyrics by A. C. Benson (1862–1925).

'Land of Hope and Glory' is also used as an anthem by England in the Commonwealth Games.

'Rule, Britannia!'

When Britain first, at Heaven's command,
Arose from out the azure main;
This was the charter of the land,
And guardian angels sung this strain:
'Rule, Britannia! rule the waves:
'Britons never will be slaves.'

'Rule, Britannia!' was probably written by the
Scottish poet James Thomson (1700–48), and
was first performed in 1740. The tune is by
the English composer Thomas Arne (1710–78).
  Like 'Land of Hope and Glory', the song is
world famous from its inclusion – with full
audience participation in the choruses – in
the Last Night of the Proms.

'Jerusalem'

And did those feet in ancient time
Walk upon England's mountains green?
And was the holy Lamb of God
On England's pleasant pastures seen?

And did the Countenance Divine
Shine forth upon our clouded hills?
And was Jerusalem builded here
Among these dark Satanic Mills?

Bring me my bow of burning gold:
Bring me my arrows of desire:
Bring me my spear: O clouds, unfold!
Bring me my chariot of fire.

I will not cease from mental fight,
Nor shall my sword sleep in my hand,
Till we have built Jerusalem,
In England's green and pleasant land.

This poem by William Blake (1757–1827) was not much known until the First World War, when it was published in an anthology of nationalist verse.

It proved so popular that in the same year, 1916, the English composer Sir Hubert Parry (1848–1918) devised a tune for it, such as could be sung at the many patriotic public meetings that were a common feature of life in wartime Britain.

In its hymn form, 'Jerusalem' is known as the unofficial anthem of the Women's Institute and, since 2004, the England cricket team; it is also frequently sung on St George's Day and at rugby matches, and is a staple of the Last Night of the Proms.

> 'If you lead a country like Britain, a strong country, a country which has taken a lead in world affairs in good times and in bad, a country that is always reliable, then you have to have a touch of iron about you.'
>
> Lady Margaret Thatcher

BRITISH SYMBOLS

The Union Jack
The distinctive British flag is a striking symbol of the United Kingdom: its red-white-and-blue design combines the cross of St George, St Andrew and St Patrick.

Originally known as the 'Union Flag', there are several – unsubstantiated – theories as to the source of the 'Jack' in its nickname.

The flag was an icon of the British Empire, and remains part of the flags of several former colonies, including Australia and New Zealand.

Recently, there have been discussions on the possible incorporation of the Welsh dragon into the British flag, which may yet add a new flavour to the current design.

'God Save The Queen'

God save our gracious Queen
Long live our noble Queen,
God save the Queen:
Send her victorious,
Happy and glorious,
Long to reign over us:
God save the Queen.

O Lord, our God, arise,
Scatter thine enemies,
And make them fall:
Confound their politics,
Frustrate their knavish tricks,
On thee our hopes we fix:
God save us all.

Thy choicest gifts in store,
On her be pleased to pour;
Long may she reign:
May she defend our laws,
And ever give us cause
To sing with heart and voice
God save the Queen.

First performed in 1745, this is the oldest national anthem still in use today.

Its adoption in Britain came about through popular usage, for it has never been officially appointed either by Act of Parliament or Royal proclamation.

The national anthem of the United Kingdom of Great Britain and Northern Ireland, its authorship is unknown, attributed to several writers, but never formally declared.

'An Englishman, even if he is alone, forms an orderly queue of one.'
George Mikes

The Tudor Rose

As Scotland uses the thistle, Ireland the shamrock and Wales the leek, so England has the Tudor rose as a heraldic symbol.

It was created when Henry VII (1457–1509) defeated Richard III (1452–1485) at the Battle of Bosworth Field in 1485, ending the Wars of the Roses.

This legendary conflict pitted the House of Lancaster (represented by a red rose) against the House of York (white rose).

The Tudor rose combines the two colours, symbolizing the marital union of Lancastrian Henry and Elizabeth of York, whom he married for good measure after the decisive military victory that made him king.

The Kilt

In Scotland, the wearing of the traditional tartan kilt lives on as strong as ever. Originating in the eighteenth century, these mid-length plaid skirts have evolved into a must-have item for any true Scot.

The tartan pattern itself, which dates from as far back as the third century, has developed into a big British icon, with the jaunty patterned cloth also finding its way into Welsh folk dress.

Amazingly, kilts were once banned in Scotland, after the defeat of Bonnie Prince Charlie (1720–88) in 1746. Those who dared to wear plaid faced a six-month jail sentence.

In November 1969, astronaut Alan Bean took tartan to the Moon; a tartan flag remains there to this day.

'The fact is that this is still the best place in the world for most things – to post a letter, go for a walk, watch television, buy a book, venture out for a drink, go to a museum, use the bank, get lost, seek help, or stand on a hillside and take in the view.'

Bill Bryson

Sir Robert Watson-Watt

(1892–1973)

WIDELY considered to be the inventor of radar, Watson-Watt studied engineering at Dundee, then part of St Andrew's University, and developed an early interest in radio waves.

After the First World War, he began investigating how aircraft could be detected by the distortion of radio signals, a project that led to the establishment of a network of radar stations, offering early advance information on aircraft flying over the English Channel.

This network, known as Chain Home and Chain Home Low, provided the vital warning intelligence that facilitated the Royal Air Force in their victory in the Battle of Britain (see page 25).

GREAT BRITISH BATTLES

The Battle of Hastings (1066)
In this famous clash, the English, led by King Harold, fought the invading army of Duke William of Normandy, aka William the Conqueror, who laid claim to the English throne.

After a ten-hour battle, which the English had been winning, an unknown archer shot Harold in the eye with an arrow. He fell, and the leaderless English fled. The story is told in the Bayeux Tapestry.

William's victory ensured the conquest of England by the Normans; his descendants still hold the throne today.

'Heart of Oak'

Come, cheer up, my lads, 'tis to glory we steer,
To add something more to this wonderful year;
To honour we call you, as freemen not slaves,
For who are as free as the sons of the waves?

Heart of oak are our ships,
Jolly tars are our men,
We always are ready;
Steady, boys, steady!
We'll fight and we'll conquer again and again. [...]

Britannia triumphant, her ships sweep the sea,
Her standard is Justice – her watchword, 'be free'.
Then cheer up, my lads, with one heart let us sing,
Our soldiers, our sailors, our statesmen, and king.

This stirring piece is the official march of the Royal Navy. It was written by David Garrick (1717–79) in 1759; the tune is by William Boyce (1711–79).

The 'oak' of the song's title is a reference to the timber from which the Royal Navy's warships of the time were built.

The 'wonderful year' of line two, meanwhile, is 1759, also known as *Annus Mirabilis* and, in British naval history, as the 'Year of Victories', from a string of remarkable British military successes against, principally, the French.

'The British nation is unique in this respect. They are the only people who like to be told how bad things are, who like to be told the worst.' Sir Winston Churchill

Admiral Horatio Lord Nelson

(1758–1805)

THE GREATEST naval commander Britain has ever produced, Norfolk-born Nelson revolutionized the way battles were fought, with daring tactics and an unprecedented level of planning.

Among many others, he won three of the most important naval victories in British history at the Nile (1798), Copenhagen (1801) and Trafalgar (1805) – despite being grievously wounded four times, including the loss of his right arm and a blinding in his right eye. It's a myth that Nelson later wore an eyepatch.

Killed at Trafalgar with victory in sight, he is commemorated in London's Trafalgar Square with Nelson's Column, a 46-metre-high structure topped with his statue. The four bronze lions guarding the base were sculpted by Sir Edwin Landseer (1802–73) – and are said to contain cannon from the defeated French fleet.

The Battle of Agincourt (25 October 1415)

Henry V of England defeated France in this seminal battle in the Hundred Years' War. It is renowned as one of England's greatest victories, as the heavily outnumbered and exhausted English army crushed the French near Agincourt in northern France.

Shakespeare's *Henry V* (*c.*1599) dramatized the battle, preceded by this stirring speech by Henry (Act IV, scene iii).

> We few, we happy few, we band of brothers;
> For he to-day that sheds his blood with me
> Shall be my brother; be he ne'er so vile,
> This day shall gentle his condition;
> And gentlemen in England now a-bed
> Shall think themselves accurs'd they were not here.

'Better wear out shoes than sheets.'

Eighteenth-century Scottish proverb

The Battle of Britain (1940)

This describes the attempt made by the German Luftwaffe during the Second World War to destroy the Royal Air Force, prior to a Nazi invasion of Britain.

The battle commenced after several European countries had fallen to the Nazis. The combination of German land and air power had defeated Holland after four days, Belgium after three weeks and France after seven weeks. Britain alone stood against the Nazis' might.

The conflict pitted Messerschmitt fighters against Hurricane and Spitfire planes. The outnumbered British pilots were helped by Britain's superior radar equipment, which gave warning of approaching raids.

The pilots' combined efforts and sacrifices (544 were killed) ultimately gave the Luftwaffe a setback from which it never really recovered.

'Never in the field of human conflict was so much owed by so many to so few.'
Sir Winston Churchill on the Battle of Britain, 1940

'The British Grenadiers'

Some talk of Alexander, and some of Hercules;
Of Hector and Lysander, and such great names as these;
But of all the world's brave heroes, there's none that can
　　compare
With a tow, row, row, row, row, row, row, for the British
　　Grenadier.

Those heroes of antiquity ne'er saw a cannon ball,
Or knew the force of powder to slay their foes withal;
But our brave boys do know it, and banish all their fears,
Sing tow, row, row, row, row, row, row, for the British
　　Grenadiers.

Probably dating from the seventeenth century, this famous
marching song has been popular for at least 200 years.

　It is still sung by the British Army today, being the
regimental quick march of the Grenadier Guards, the
Honourable Artillery Company and the Royal Regiment of
Fusiliers.

Sir Arthur Wellesley,
Duke of Wellington

(1769–1852)

TWICE Prime Minister, this Dublin-born army general is best known for defeating Napoleon (1769–1821) at the legendary Battle of Waterloo (1815).

Knighted after a victory at Assaye (1803), in 1808 Wellington led the British, Portuguese and Spanish armies in the Peninsular War (1808–14), to great success.

When Napoleon returned post-abdication and threatened Europe again in 1815, Wellington was appointed a commander of the allied armies, and famously triumphed against the former French Emperor at Waterloo, becoming a hero throughout the continent.

'English people apparently queue up as a sort of hobby.'

Calvin Trillin

LOCATION, LOCATION, LOCATION

The White Cliffs of Dover

In some places over 100 metres (300 feet) high, these chalk cliffs run for about 16 kilometres (10 miles) along the south coast of England as part of the South Downs, and include such landmarks as the Seven Sisters and Beachy Head.

In 1941, they became a symbol of the hope for peace in the song '(There'll Be Bluebirds Over) The White Cliffs of Dover', written by Walter Kent and Nat Burton, and memorably recorded by Vera Lynn in 1942.

> 'England has four seasons. But do we have to have them in one day?'
>
> Oscar Wilde

'The White Cliffs'

I have loved England, dearly and deeply,
Since that first morning, shining and pure,
The white cliffs of Dover I saw rising steeply
Out of the sea that once made her secure.

This is an extract from the first stanza of a verse novel
by Alice Duer Miller (1874–1942).

Published in 1940, *The White Cliffs* to some extent
influenced the US decision to join the Second World
War, and sold nearly a million copies.

St Paul's Cathedral

Situated on Ludgate Hill in the City of
London, St Paul's is famed for its domed
roof, and the Whispering Gallery inside it.

The St Paul's we know today was designed by
Sir Christopher Wren (1632–1723) and built between 1675

and 1710, after its predecessor was destroyed in the Great Fire of London.

The organ, completed in 1695, was once played by Mendelssohn.

Over the years, the cathedral has played host to many seminal events, such as the funerals of Admiral Lord Nelson and Sir Winston Churchill; services marking the end of the World Wars; the 1981 wedding of Prince Charles and Lady Diana Spencer; the Service of Remembrance and Commemoration for 11 September 2001; and, most recently, the Golden Jubilee of Her Majesty the Queen.

Loch Ness

Over 37 kilometres (23 miles) long, a mile wide and 230 metres (754 feet) at its deepest, Loch Ness (from the Scottish Gaelic, *Loch Nis*) is the largest lake on the Great Glen rift valley in Scotland.

It is best known for the 'sightings' of the legendary Loch Ness Monster. The first documented sighting was in 1871, although there have been legends about the loch since medieval times.

Popular belief has fluctuated since a hoax photograph brought 'Nessie' to the world's attention in 1933. Possibly a plesiosaur which has survived from prehistoric times, Nessie has made fewer appearances recently.

Despite extensive investigations, no physical evidence of the monster's existence has ever been uncovered.

The Lake District

This National Park is England's largest and covers 2,292 square kilometres (885 square miles).

It has over fourteen lakes and tarns, smooth U-shaped valleys, steep and sharp ridges, plus England's highest mountain, Scafell Pike at 978 metres (3,210 feet).

There have been people in the Lake District since the end of the last Ice Age.

The dramatic landscape has inspired the likes of poet William Wordsworth (1770–1850), who spent most of his life in the area and penned this famous 1804 verse about a visit to Glencoyne Park.

'I Wandered Lonely as a Cloud'

(also known as 'The Daffodils')

I wandered lonely as a cloud
That floats on high o'er vales and hills,
When all at once I saw a crowd,
A host, of golden daffodils;
Beside the lake, beneath the trees,
Fluttering and dancing in the breeze.

Continuous as the stars that shine
And twinkle on the milky way,
They stretched in never-ending line
Along the margin of a bay:
Ten thousand saw I at a glance,
Tossing their heads in sprightly dance.

The waves beside them danced; but they
Out-did the sparkling waves in glee:
A poet could not but be gay,
In such a jocund company:
I gazed – and gazed – but little thought
What wealth the show to me had brought:

For oft, when on my couch I lie
In vacant or in pensive mood,
They flash upon that inward eye
Which is the bliss of solitude;
And then my heart with pleasure fills,
And dances with the daffodils.

The Houses of Parliament

The site of Parliament has been a centre of power for over a millennium. A royal residence until 1512, when Henry VIII (1491–1547) moved out, it remains a royal palace and is often called 'the Palace of Westminster'.

On 16 October 1834, a fire tore through Parliament, destroying nearly everything. Sir Charles Barry (1795–1860) designed the current building, which was completed in 1870.

Barry's Gothic vision incorporated the Clock Tower, popularly known as Big Ben – though that nickname in fact refers to the bell. Its chimes first rang out in July 1859.

Bizarrely enough, the Clock Tower has a Prison Room, where members of both Houses can be sent for misbehaving. It was last used in 1880, when Charles Bradlaugh MP refused to swear the oath of allegiance to Queen Victoria.

The oldest part of Parliament is Westminster Hall, the walls of which were built in 1097 on the orders of William the Conqueror's son. It has hosted numerous historical events, most notably the trials of Sir William Wallace (1305), the Gunpowder Plot conspirators (1606) and King Charles I (1649), and received the abdication of Richard II in 1399.

Charles Darwin

(1809–82)

—————————

DARWIN began his academic career studying Theology at Christ's College, Cambridge; however, his fascination with insects, plants and geological samples was observed by botany professor John Stevens Henslow (1796–1861), who arranged for Darwin to travel as a naturalist on board HMS *Beagle*.

The voyage took five years. During that time, Darwin contracted a tropical illness – but he also returned with a collection of specimens and observations.

He published several early works based on his discoveries and in the 1840s developed his most renowned theory, that all species share a few common ancestors. *The Origin of Species* (1859) was fiercely attacked for its anti-Creationist hypotheses, but remains the foundation for all modern studies on evolution.

THE BRITISH MONARCHY

Shakespeare's Histories

Towards the end of the sixteenth century, William Shakespeare began writing a series of history plays, focusing on twelfth- to sixteenth-century English monarchs.

This noble speech is from *Richard II* (1595; Act II, scene i).

> This royal throne of kings, this scepter'd isle,
> This earth of majesty, this seat of Mars,
> This other Eden, demi-paradise,
> This fortress built by Nature for herself
> Against infection and the hand of war,

This happy breed of men, this little world,
This precious stone set in the silver sea,
Which serves it in the office of a wall,
Or as a moat defensive to a house,
Against the envy of less happier lands,
This blessèd plot, this earth, this realm, this England,
This nurse, this teeming womb of royal kings,
Fear'd by their breed and famous by their birth,
Renowned for their deeds as far from home,
For Christian service and true chivalry.

Unusual Royal Appointments

Many of these posts are now ceremonial, but a good number – such as the Royal Goat Herd – are not.

- Gold Stick (in Waiting) / Silver Stick (in Waiting) – in Tudor times, the personal bodyguards to the Sovereign; now largely ceremonial, the two Gold

Sticks and one Silver Stick are senior officers of the Household Cavalry
- Royal Goat Herd
- Royal Herbstrewer
- Keeper of the Royal Philatelic Collection
- Manager of the Royal Studs
- Royal Swan Keeper
- Queen's Champion – an hereditary office held by the Dymokes of Scrivelsby, Lincolnshire, since the fourteenth century
- Surveyor of the Queen's Pictures
- Queen's Piper – whose principal duty is to play the bagpipes beneath Her Majesty's window every weekday at 9 a.m. Beats an alarm clock . . .

'What is our task? To make Britain a fit country for heroes to live in.'

David Lloyd George

The Queen's Garden Parties

These relatively informal occasions, attended by Her Majesty the Queen, happen four times a year. One party is held at the Palace of Holyroodhouse in Edinburgh, Scotland, with the remaining three hosted at Buckingham Palace in London – the monarch's official residence since 1837.

The parties are organized for members of the public who have contributed to society – but you can't just turn up or beg for an invite if you think you should be there. Instead, nominations for invitations are made through Lord Lieutenants, and various other official bodies.

Queen Victoria began the Garden Parties in the 1860s. Today, over 30,000 people attend them annually – it's just as well Buckingham Palace has seventy-eight bathrooms!

At each garden party, around 27,000 cups of tea, 20,000 sandwiches and 20,000 slices of cake are consumed.

'I Vow to Thee, My Country'

I vow to thee, my country, all earthly things above,
Entire and whole and perfect, the service of my love,
The love that asks no question: the love that stands the
test,
That lays upon the altar the dearest and the best;
The love that never falters, the love that pays the price,
The love that makes undaunted the final sacrifice.

And there's another country, I've heard of long ago –
Most dear to them that love her, most great to them that
know;
We may not count her armies, we may not see her King;
Her fortress is a faithful heart, her pride is suffering;
And soul by soul and silently her shining bounds
increase,

And her ways are ways of gentleness and all her paths are
    Peace.

This hymn was originally a poem by Sir Cecil Spring-Rice
(1859–1918), which was set to music in 1921 by the English
composer Gustav Holst (1874–1934).
    It was a favourite of Diana, Princess of Wales (1961–97),
and played at both her 1981 wedding and 1997 funeral.

'What the British must never believe about themselves
is that they are good at games, strong in adversity, but
lousy in bed. It is a myth invented by jealous foreigners.'
                                                    Gerald McKnight

Charles Babbage

(1791–1871)

———————

A PIONEER of computing, Babbage studied mathematics at Cambridge University.

In the 1820s, Babbage designed and constructed his 'Difference Engine', a machine that could perform mathematical calculations. Later came his revolutionary 'Analytical Engine', a device intended to perform any calculation using punched cards.

Today, parts of his uncompleted mechanisms are exhibited in the London Science Museum.

In 1991, a Difference Engine was assembled from Babbage's original plans. Incredibly, it was fully operative.

> 'There's nothing the British like better than a bloke who comes from nowhere, makes it, and then gets clobbered.'
>
> Melvyn Bragg

Sir Tim Berners-Lee

(1955–)

B ERNERS-LEE, born in London, graduated from Queen's College, Oxford, in 1976. Thirteen years later, he invented the World Wide Web.

This was made available on the Internet in 1991, and since then Berners-Lee has continued to perfect its design, founding the World Wide Web Consortium at the Massachusetts Institute of Technology in America.

He has been the recipient of several international awards including the Millennium Technology Prize, and was knighted in 2004.

'Our [British] summers are often, though beautiful for verdure, so cold, that they are rather cold winters.'

Horace Walpole

AFTERNOON TEA

It is believed that Anna Russell, Duchess of Bedford (1783–1857), one of Queen Victoria's ladies-in-waiting, created this quintessentially British tradition in the mid nineteenth century.

Since the evening meal was served around 8 p.m., she often found she was peckish in the afternoon. She began requesting a pot of tea with bread and butter.

Soon, she started inviting her friends to join her, the menu grew more lavish and the practice quickly became commonplace in wealthy houses up and down the country.

| 'Oh, to be in England.' | Robert Browning |

The Traditional Spread

Typically, a pot of tea accompanies an assortment of thin cucumber, salmon and cress sandwiches, followed by scones – a Scottish quick bread that takes its name from the Stone of Destiny (or Scone), where Scottish kings were once crowned – with jam and clotted cream, and a selection of cakes.

The tradition is still upheld in select hotels in Britain, for example at The Ritz, London, where tea may be taken in the beautiful Palm Court.

How to Make the Perfect Cup of Tea

There are countless different schools of thought on the various stages of brewing up.

Nonetheless, here are some traditional 'do's and 'don't's of tea etiquette.

- Ideally, before the tea is added, the pot should be warmed with boiling water, which is then poured away.
- Boiling water should be added to the tea, not the other way round, and then be left to brew for approximately three to five minutes.
- A little milk should be poured into each cup before straining the tea.
- The little finger should be gently raised while lifting the teacup – not for affectation, but to ensure balance.
- Tea must not be stirred, but gently folded away from you.
- Most Britons drink their tea with milk or, occasionally, a slice of lemon (but never, ever both). Cream has no place in tea!

The History of Tea

Although regarded as the most British of beverages, tea did not in fact arrive on British shores until the mid seventeenth century when Portuguese and Dutch traders began importing it to Europe.

Interestingly, it was the coffee houses of London that first popularized the drink – by 1700, over 500 coffee houses offered tea and it became fashionable across all classes.

King Charles II (1630–1685) imposed heavy taxes on its import, which led to smuggling and the adulteration of tea leaves with other substances.

When the taxes were lifted, tea clippers were developed by the East India Company to facilitate quicker imports, the most famous of which is the *Cutty Sark*, built in 1868.

British companies continue to play a leading role in the global tea trade to this day.

John Logie Baird

(1888–1946)

THIS Scottish engineer is renowned for being the first person to demonstrate a working television.

He showed signs of genius from an early age, setting up a telephone exchange from his bedroom to those of his friends across the street.

After the First World War, he turned his hand to creating a TV and, on 26 January 1926, he gave the world's first demonstration to an audience of scientists in an attic room in London.

Forming the Baird Television Development Company, he achieved the first transatlantic television transmission between London and New York.

He is also credited with being the first to demonstrate colour television.

ENTERTAINMENT

Punch and Judy

This traditional puppetry show had its greatest success with Victorian audiences, when coastal holidays in Britain were popular.

Punch, thought to have developed from *commedia dell'arte*, is characterized by an enormous nose, hunched back and a club or stick, which he uses to beat his squabbling wife, Judy. The tragicomic plot they enact first emerged in the late eighteenth century.

Despite a recent decline, the puppets and the red-and-white striped stalls that form their stage remain iconic images of British seaside entertainment.

Doctor Who

Produced by the BBC, the award-winning *Doctor Who* is the longest-running science-fiction TV show in history.

It follows the adventures of an enigmatic time traveller known as 'The Doctor', who roams the universe in his ship, the TARDIS, which appears from the outside as a blue police phone box from the 1950s, but in fact has a vast interior.

The title character, capable of regenerating himself and taking on new human forms, was played by various actors in the original run from 1963 to 1989, and is currently portrayed by Scotsman David Tennant.

Executive producer Russell T. Davies resurrected the programme in 2004. Now filmed in Wales, it remains, as Caitlin Moran of *The Times* put it, 'quintessential to being British'.

Indeed, the programme has become a national institution, with many of its quirks and phrases seeping into common parlance.

The chilling theme music, coupled with the harrowing alien creatures, most notably the Daleks, are instantly recognizable all around the world.

Morris Dancing

Morris dancing is a form of English folk dance. Its exact origins are unknown, but references extend back 600 years, making it one of the oldest continuing traditions of rural England.

The most common form of morris is known as Cotswold, named after the region of England in which it originated. The style of the dance alters from region to region – with some sides using handkerchiefs, while others clash sticks or swords.

Today, morris dancing is still performed on occasions such as Plough Monday, Easter and May Day (see page 65).

The Morris Ring, an organization founded in 1934 by six revival sides, aims to promote morris dancing and safeguard its traditions. Somewhat unbelievably, it is now an international organization with several hundred member-sides.

James Bond

British secret agent James Bond was created in 1952 by the writer Ian Fleming (1908–1964), and first appeared in the novel *Casino Royale* (1953). The character has since become a global household name – along with his trademark drink ('Vodka Martini . . . shaken, not stirred').

It was film producers Harry Saltzman (1915–1994) and Albert 'Cubby' Broccoli (1909–1996) who brought 007 to international audiences and elevated him to cult status. The first adaptation – *Dr No* – appeared in 1962, starring Sean Connery as Bond.

To date, six actors (Connery, George Lazenby, Roger Moore, Timothy Dalton, Pierce Brosnan and Daniel Craig) have played Bond in the official movies, which have made over $4 billion.

Impressively, Bond is second only to the equally British franchise Harry Potter as the highest grossing film series of all time.

The Two Ronnies

Ronnie Barker (1929–2005) and Ronnie Corbett (1930–) were the British comic legends behind this TV show, which was the dominant comedy programme of the 1980s.

The seminal sketch show featured the tour de force in wordplay, 'Four Candles', which remains one of the most popular British comedy sketches of all time.

It is set in an ironmonger's shop, where the assistant confuses a request for 'fork handles', and instead supplies four candles …

With that brilliant opening, the hilarity and befuddlement have only just begun.

> 'Ask any man what nationality he would prefer to be, and ninety-nine out of a hundred will tell you that they would prefer to be Englishmen.'
>
> Cecil Rhodes

The Eurovision Song Contest

This annual European music competition was dreamed up by the European Broadcasting Union in the 1950s. The first Eurovision subsequently took place on 24 May 1956 in Switzerland.

It was a British journalist, George Campey, who coined the word 'Eurovision' in the London *Evening Standard* in 1951.

To date, the United Kingdom has triumphed five times, with these classic tunes.

'Puppet on a String' (Sandie Shaw, 1967)
'Boom Bang-a-Bang' (Lulu, 1969)
'Save Your Kisses For Me' (Brotherhood of Man, 1976)
'Making Your Mind Up' (Bucks Fizz, 1981)
'Love Shine a Light' (Katrina and the Waves, 1997)

> 'I like the English. They have the most rigid code of immorality in the world.'
>
> Malcolm Bradbury

Alexander Graham Bell

(1847–1922)

BORN in Edinburgh to a deaf mother and a father who studied elocution and speech, Bell was fascinated by the education of deaf people. After attending Edinburgh University, he trained under his father's instruction in the practice of removing speech impediments.

Moving to Boston, America, in 1872, it was his interest in hearing and speech that led to his development of the 'electrical speech machine', a device capable of transmitting sound by electricity. We now call this device 'the telephone'.

It is believed that Bell considered his most famous invention to be an intrusion on his work – and refused to have a telephone in his study.

LITERATURE

'If—'

Although written in 1896, this poem by Rudyard Kipling (1865–1936) first appeared in his short story 'Brother Square Toes', part of his 1910 collection *Rewards and Fairies*.

It helped to cement his reputation as the country's unofficial poet laureate, one of many honours he refused, although he accepted the Nobel Prize in Literature in 1907.

In a countrywide poll organized by BBC TV's *Bookworm* programme in 1995, 'If—' was voted the Nation's Favourite Poem.

If you can keep your head when all about you
Are losing theirs and blaming it on you,
If you can trust yourself when all men doubt you
But make allowance for their doubting too,
If you can wait and not be tired by waiting,
Or being lied about, don't deal in lies,
Or being hated, don't give way to hating,
And yet don't look too good, nor talk too wise:
If you can dream – and not make dreams your master,
If you can think – and not make thoughts your aim;
If you can meet with Triumph and Disaster
And treat those two impostors just the same;
If you can bear to hear the truth you've spoken
Twisted by knaves to make a trap for fools,
Or watch the things you gave your life to, broken,
And stoop and build 'em up with worn-out tools:
If you can make one heap of all your winnings
And risk it all on one turn of pitch-and-toss,
And lose, and start again at your beginnings

And never breathe a word about your loss;
If you can force your heart and nerve and sinew
To serve your turn long after they are gone,
And so hold on when there is nothing in you
Except the Will which says to them: 'Hold on!'
If you can talk with crowds and keep your virtue,
Or walk with Kings – nor lose the common touch,
If neither foes nor loving friends can hurt you;
If all men count with you, but none too much,
If you can fill the unforgiving minute
With sixty seconds' worth of distance run,
Yours is the Earth and everything that's in it,
And – which is more – you'll be a Man, my son!

'The British do not expect happiness. I had the impression [...] that they do not want to be happy; they want to be right.'

Quentin Crisp

William Shakespeare

(1564–1616)

W IDELY considered to be the greatest writer in the English language, Shakespeare was born and died in Stratford-on-Avon, but his major writing took place in London.

His plays were first noted in the early 1590s, and he penned roughly two a year until 1611. Many of his best-known tragedies were completed in the early seventeenth century, including *Hamlet* (1600–1), *Othello* (1604), *Macbeth* (1605–6) and *King Lear* (1605–6).

Shakespeare was a shareholder in the Globe Theatre (built in 1599). Many of his plays were acted there by the Chamberlain's Men. They became the King's Men in 1604 by Royal command of King James I (1566–1625).

Shakespeare's thirty-seven plays were published in the *First Folio* in 1623: a unique tribute to a unique talent. He also wrote 154 sonnets – one of which is reproduced here.

'Sonnet 18'

Shall I compare thee to a Summer's day?
Thou art more lovely and more temperate:
Rough winds do shake the darling buds of May,
And Summer's lease hath all too short a date:
Sometime too hot the eye of heaven shines,
And oft' is his gold complexion dimm'd;
And every fair from fair sometime declines,
By chance or nature's changing course untrimm'd:
But thy eternal Summer shall not fade
Nor lose possession of that fair thou owest;
Nor shall Death brag thou wanderest in his shade,
When in eternal lines to time thou growest:
So long as men can breathe, or eyes can see,
So long lives this, and this gives life to thee.

The Big Read

In 2003, the BBC undertook a search to find the UK's favourite book. Here is their top ten, as chosen by the British public, three quarters of a million of whom voted.

1. *The Lord of the Rings*, J. R. R. Tolkien
2. *Pride and Prejudice*, Jane Austen
3. *His Dark Materials*, Philip Pullman
4. *The Hitchhiker's Guide to the Galaxy*, Douglas Adams
5. *Harry Potter and the Goblet of Fire*, J. K. Rowling
6. *To Kill a Mockingbird*, Harper Lee
7. *Winnie the Pooh*, A. A. Milne
8. *Nineteen Eighty-Four*, George Orwell
9. *The Lion, the Witch and the Wardrobe*, C. S. Lewis
10. *Jane Eyre*, Charlotte Brontë

> 'The British have an umbilical cord which has never been cut and through which tea flows constantly.'
>
> Marlene Dietrich

Robert Burns

(1759–96)

———————————

BORN in Alloway, Ayrshire, Burns is considered Scotland's national bard. He was the son of a poor tenant farmer, but received a good education. Following his father's death in 1784, he continued farming, but also started writing poems in his native Scots.

A decision to emigrate to Jamaica led him to publish *Poems, chiefly in the Scottish Dialect* (1786) to finance the trip. Known as the Kilmarnock Edition, the second impression (1787) sold 3,000 copies on the first day. Burns stayed in Scotland.

He published his last major poem, *Tam O'Shanter*, in 1790, and gave up farming the year after.

Burns Night (see page 67) celebrates his life and work.

'O, My Luve is Like a Red, Red Rose'

O, my luve is like a red, red rose,
That's newly sprung in June.
O, my luve is like a melodie,
That's sweetly play'd in tune.

'The Soldier'
Poet Rupert Brooke (1887–1915) is regarded
as typifying the doomed 'golden youth' of
the First World War.

'The Soldier', one of five 'War Sonnets',
appeared in Brooke's posthumous collection
1914 and Other Poems (1915), which
established him as one of the best-known
poets of the era.

If I should die, think only this of me:
That there's some corner of a foreign field
That is for ever England. There shall be
In that rich earth a richer dust concealed;
A dust whom England bore, shaped, made aware,
Gave, once, her flowers to love, her ways to roam,
A body of England's, breathing English air,
Washed by the rivers, blest by suns of home.

And think, this heart, all evil shed away,
A pulse in the eternal mind, no less,
Gives somewhere back the thoughts by England given;
Her sights and sounds; dreams happy as her day;
And laughter, learnt of friends; and gentleness,
In hearts at peace, under an English heaven.

> 'For he himself has said it,
> And it's greatly to his credit,
> That he is an Englishman.'   W. S. Gilbert, *HMS Pinafore*

BRITISH CELEBRATIONS

May Day

Celebrated on 1 May, this is probably the most ancient festival in Britain. It welcomes the coming of summer.

In medieval times, young men and women went out into the woods to gather branches of may (hawthorn), flowers and other greenery to decorate their houses to mark the end of winter.

Many places crowned a May queen, who would preside over the festivities. These included dancing around a maypole, morris dancing, athletic games and archery contests.

In some places, plays were staged which featured traditional characters such as St George, Robin Hood and Aunt Sally, who was played by a man dressed as a woman.

In the north of England, some villages still practice well dressing. Large framed panels with elaborate mosaic-like pictures made of flower petals, seeds, leaves, bark, berries and moss are placed beside the well.

Hogmanay

Celebrated on New Year's Eve, 31 December, this Scottish festival appeared in the 1790s after Christmas was virtually banned by the Kirk.

Many people would clean their houses, pay their debts, and take out the ashes to prepare for the New Year. They really knew how to party.

Nowadays, people hold a get-together for family and friends. Immediately after midnight, everyone sings 'Auld Land Syne' by Robert Burns.

> Should auld acquaintance be forgot, and never
>   brought to mind?
> Should auld acquaintance be forgot, and auld lang
>   syne?

For auld lang syne, my dear, for auld lang syne,
We'll take a cup o' kindness yet, for auld lang syne.

'First footing' – the first person to enter the house after midnight, on New Year's Day – is still common in Scotland.

To ensure good luck for the coming year, the first footer should be male, dark and bring one or all of a lump of coal, salt, a black bun, shortbread and whisky.

Burns Night

Celebrated in honour of the Scottish poet Robert Burns (see page 62), this is an annual knees-up held on 25 January.

Scots gather to eat a traditional Burns Supper of haggis, neaps (mashed turnips) and tatties (mashed potatoes). They drink Scotch and recite Robert Burns's poetry, tell stories of his life and sing settings of his poems. The idea is that everyone should take a turn to perform.

There are two traditional toasts given: the Immortal Memory (of Burns) and the Toast to the Lassies.

The first Burns Night occurred on 25 January 1801 on the anniversary of Robert Burns's birthday.

St George's Day

This has fallen on 23 April since 1222; St George has officially been the patron saint of England since the fourteenth century.

Despite this longevity, the English do not make a great fuss about St George's Day – you might see the odd chap wearing a rose in his buttonhole, there may be a concert of English music staged, but that's about it.

The English flag – a red cross on a white background – was originally the emblem of St George. During the twelfth-century Crusades, Richard the Lionheart (1157–1199) adopted it for the nation.

In Shakespeare's *Henry V* (c.1599; Act III, scene i), King Henry invokes the saint in this rousing pre-battle speech.

Once more unto the breach, dear friends, once more;
Or close the wall up with our English dead.
In peace there's nothing so becomes a man
As modest stillness and humility:
But when the blast of war blows in our ears,
Then imitate the action of the tiger;
Stiffen the sinews, summon up the blood,
Disguise fair nature with hard-favour'd rage;
Then lend the eye a terrible aspect;
Let pry through the portage of the head
Like the brass cannon; let the brow o'erwhelm it
As fearfully as doth a galled rock
O'erhang and jutty his confounded base,
Swill'd with the wild and wasteful ocean.
Now set the teeth and stretch the nostril wide,
Hold hard the breath and bend up every spirit
To his full height. On, on, you noblest English.
Whose blood is fet from fathers of war-proof!
Fathers that, like so many Alexanders,

Have in these parts from morn till even fought
And sheathed their swords for lack of argument:
Dishonour not your mothers; now attest
That those whom you call'd fathers did beget you.
Be copy now to men of grosser blood,
And teach them how to war. And you, good yeoman,
Whose limbs were made in England, show us here
The mettle of your pasture; let us swear
That you are worth your breeding; which I doubt not;
For there is none of you so mean and base,
That hath not noble lustre in your eyes.
I see you stand like greyhounds in the slips,
Straining upon the start. The game's afoot:
Follow your spirit, and upon this charge
Cry 'God for Harry, England, and Saint George!'

Armistice Day

At the eleventh hour of the eleventh day of the eleventh
month in 1918, the First World War ended.

In 1919, King George V dedicated 11 November to the

remembrance of members of the armed forces killed during conflict; it became known as Remembrance Day, and is today honoured in the UK on Remembrance Sunday.

A two-minute silence is held at 11 a.m., with ceremonies throughout the country at war memorials, and specifically at the Cenotaph in London. Artificial poppies are worn – a symbol inspired by the 1915 poem 'In Flanders Field' by John McCrae.

The 'Last Post' is played, and often the 'Scottish Bagpiper's Lament'.

Bonfire Night

A fixture in the British calendar since 1605, 5 November is also known as Guy Fawkes Night, and commemorates the Gunpowder Plot to blow up the Houses of Parliament.

The conspirators were a group of Catholic gentry, led by Robert Catesby, who were enraged at the ill treatment of Catholics in England.

The plot was uncovered when Guy Fawkes was caught red-handed beneath Parliament with thirty-six barrels of gunpowder. He and the rest of the gang were executed for treason in March 1607.

To this day, before the State Opening of Parliament, the Yeomen of the Guard traditionally search its cellars to check for explosives.

Bonfire Night began on the very evening the plot was foiled, with people lighting bonfires to celebrate the King's deliverance.

Since then, it's become an annual event, with bonfires, fireworks and burning effigies of Mr Fawkes all part of the celebrations. The occasion is immortalized in this nursery rhyme.

> Remember, remember the fifth of November:
> Gunpowder, treason and plot.
> We see no reason
> Why gunpowder treason
> Should ever be forgot!

Sir Alexander Fleming

(1881–1955)

CREDITED with the creation of a substance that has saved millions of lives, Fleming was born in Ayrshire, Scotland and attended St Mary's Medical School in London.

In 1928, while studying an influenza virus, he observed that a mould, which had unexpectedly matured on a culture plate, had prevented the growth of staphylococci around itself.

He named the substance penicillin. The discovery altered the face of modern medicine, proving the first step in the development of other important antibiotics.

Fleming was awarded the Nobel Prize in Medicine in 1945, shared with Howard Florey (1898–1968) and Ernst Chain (1906–1979), who developed a powder form of the medicine.

BRITISH TRANSPORT

The Steam-Powered Locomotive Train

Originally conceived by the Cornishman Richard Trevithick (1771–1833) in 1804, this is one of the most significant British inventions of all time.

The emergence of the steam train ushered in a new age of travel that had infiltrated the whole of Britain by the end of the nineteenth century, and was reproduced around the world to great success.

Before Trevithick's invention, horses and carts were the major form of transport. Steam trains – and the railways that were built for them – revolutionized travel for industry and people alike, and played a key role in the vast economic growth that Britain enjoyed in the nineteenth century.

The Motor Car

Britain dominated the automobile industry in the mid twentieth century, providing 52 per cent of the world's exported vehicles.

One of the most famous British motor cars is the Morris Minor, which was the first car to combine economy with efficiency, making the vehicle available to people from all spectrums of society.

The motor car faced initial protest from the general public, with concerns that the automobile spoiled roads and frightened cavalry, and was altogether dangerous.

Motor-enthusiasts prevailed, however, and the motor car industry remains an economic stalwart of Britain to this day.

Rolls-Royce

Formed in April 1906 by Sir Henry Royce (1863–1933) and the Honourable Charles Rolls (1877–1910), this great British company began life simply as a car production firm, Royce having built his first motor car in 1904.

The Rolls-Royce launch vehicle, the Silver Ghost, was acclaimed as the 'best car in the world' by *Autocar* in 1907.

With the advent of the First World War, Royce turned his attention to the aeroplane engine. His subsequent creation, the Eagle, not only triumphed in the conflict, but also powered the first direct transatlantic flight.

It was another Rolls-Royce engine that played a key role in Britain's dominance in the Battle of Britain (see page 25). Royce's Merlin engine drove both the Hurricane and Spitfire planes during the Second World War.

Britain's air supremacy during the Blitz was vital to the Allies' campaign in the global combat. Without it, ultimate victory may well have escaped us.

> 'Strive for perfection in everything you do. Take the best that exists and make it better. When it does not exist, design it.'
> Sir Henry Royce

Hackney Carriages (Taxi Cabs)

You can't go far in the English capital without spotting one of these famed black cars, unmistakeable by their distinctive design.

Technically embellished by their unique turning abilities, these four-door saloons have a turning circle of only 7.6 metres (25 feet) and can fit up to five passengers.

There are 21,000 currently in rotation around London, manned by a fleet of highly trained British cabbies.

Since 1851, taxi drivers have had to pass a rigorous exam called 'The Knowledge', which tests their ability to navigate London's streets without the aid of a map or radio, before they receive their licence – by far the most demanding course for a taxi driver anywhere in the world.

> 'Smile at us, pay us, pass us; but do not quite forget,
> For we are the people of England, that never has
> spoken yet.'
> G. K. Chesterton

The Routemaster Bus

An iconic vision of London, these red double-decker buses have been loved for their striking colour and design ever since first production in the 1950s.

The original 'hop on, hop off' buses with the conductor and open rear door were officially phased out from 2003.

However, due to the immense nostalgia felt for the design, two working Routemaster 'heritage routes' remain in operation in the city.

The London Underground

A world-famous engineering feat, the Tube is renowned for its roundel logo and art-deco-style map, the latter designed by Harry Beck in 1931.

The brainchild of Charles Pearson in 1845, the Tube first opened for business on 10 January 1863 with just one line, the Metropolitan. Its existence was not universally applauded: in 1862, *The Times* described Pearson's idea as an 'insult to common sense'.

The London Underground was the world's only steam-driven underground railway and the first electrified underground railway. Its expansion was aided by the city's exemplary geological make-up: the London clay fortuitously turned out to be the perfect material in which to dig the Tube's tunnels.

Today, it's impossible to imagine London without the Underground. The network now boasts twelve lines and has over 407 kilometres (253 miles) of tunnels snaking under the city, through which over 1 billion passengers travel every year.

> 'The English never smash in a face. They merely refrain from asking it to dinner.'
> Margaret Halsey

Isambard Kingdom Brunel

(1806–59)

ONE OF the most resourceful and intrepid engineers of the nineteenth century, Brunel is probably best remembered for his work on the Great Western Railway, which links London to Bristol.

In addition, Brunel designed several steam-powered ships, the *Great Western* being the first to offer a transatlantic crossing. One such ship was named *Great Britain*.

At the age of twenty-four, his ingenuity also won him the competition to design the Clifton Suspension Bridge, which stands today as a symbol of Bristol and a memorial to the great engineer, who died before its completion.

'I just think British music is the best.' Sir Paul McCartney

THE INDUSTRIAL REVOLUTION

This global sea change began in Britain in the eighteenth century, and is still impacting around the world today.

It marked a shift from manual labour and agriculture to a machine age of industry, which saw a huge increase in the number of people employed in industrial manufacturing. Machines in factories replaced the home production or small workshops of the previous period.

The knock-on effect was that the population became dense in towns and cities, whereas previously people had lived in rural homes.

Powered by water or steam-fuelled by coal, the machines allowed production to be increased and speeded up. Consequently, there was massive economic growth for those in possession of the improved technology.

In history, there is only one other revolution that has had such a significant and widespread effect: that of the Neolithic Revolution in the Stone Age, when the hunter-gatherer society became more complex.

The British Empire

As Britain was at the forefront of the Industrial Revolution, it was able to use the vast wealth it accrued to develop a world empire that, at its height, covered 25 per cent of the Earth's land surface and had jurisdiction over 458 million people: the largest empire of all time.

'In peacetime the British may have many faults; but so far an inferiority complex has not been one of them.'

Lord Gladwyn

The Revolution's Pioneers

Sir Richard Arkwright (1733–92) is considered by many to have instigated and facilitated the Industrial Revolution. Fascinated by the mechanics of the textiles industry, in 1775 he patented an improved spinning machine. His Spinning-Frame was capable of producing a stronger yarn and required less physical labour to operate.

Constantly driven to improve efficiency, he developed a horse-drawn spinning mill at Preston and was also quick to embrace the new steam engine developed by James Watt.

James Watt (1736–1819) was one of the foremost inventors of the era. His work on the steam engine was one of the crucial innovations that enabled the Industrial Revolution.

It was Watt who first used the term 'horsepower'. The International System of Units' unit of power is named in the Scotsman's honour.

George Stephenson (1781–1848) was known as the 'father of railways'. He is credited with building the world's first public railway to use steam locomotives, establishing the Stockton and Darlington Railway in 1825.

He is also famous for developing the Rocket (pictured), the most advanced locomotive of the era, which won the 1829 Rainhill Trials and was a driving force in the Industrial Revolution.

A great Victorian mechanical engineer, Stephenson paved the way for other great inventors of the time – and his legacy survives in the standard gauges still used by railway lines in Britain to this day.

'Names are not always what they seem. The common Welsh name BZJXXLLWCP is pronounced Jackson.'

Mark Twain

BEST BRITISH QUIRKS

Queuing

The Great British Tradition: a finely tuned system of etiquette representing all that is good, fair and civilized about the United Kingdom. British people form queues with an elegant effortlessness unseen in any other culture.

If you want to experience a quintessentially British sensation, walk into any post office and barge right into the middle of the queue – the mood of suppressed rage is incomparable.

Weather

Dr Johnson once wrote, 'When two Englishmen meet, their first talk is of the weather.' He's very nearly right. When a day turns from rain to shine every few hours, there is always something to talk about.

While weather may be construed as a banal topic of conversation in any other country, in Britain it is practically a national pastime.

Tea Drinking

It is rare to pass the threshold of any British household for long before you are offered this great British classic, the cup of tea.

With the average Briton knocking back three cups a day, it is clear that the popularity of this staple hot drink is still going strong.

Indeed, as you read this there are probably a dozen heated debates going on around the country about the correct way to serve it, and the eternal question: do you put the milk in first, or last? (See page 46 for the answer!)

Celebrating Failure: The British Underdog

It is a peculiar nation that chooses to celebrate its losers as well as its winners. Yet the affection for the 'underdog' character has become part of Britain's cultural DNA, with the value of failing and going down with a smile on your face almost as important as winning.

Take *Only Fools and Horses,* for example, one of Britain's best-loved television shows, with Del Boy's hapless line, 'This time next year we'll be millionaires…'

Manners

British manners are considered to be the most formal in the world.

For instance, should your meal in a restaurant not be up to scratch, your complaint would naturally begin with an apology: 'I'm terribly sorry, but my steak seems to have been burnt to a crisp.'

Try saying 'please', 'thank you' or 'sorry' after every sentence, and you'll be talking like a native in no time.

The Stiff Upper Lip

Britons have often been accused of coldness and reserve – for example, in preferring the classic handshake as a greeting over continental-style kisses.

This tendency to remain detached goes back a long way into the national consciousness, born of the public-school 'stiff-upper-lip' ethos, where a boy stands up straight and doesn't blubber in the face of adversity.

Despite inevitable changes in British society, the power of this natural stoicism remains strong, seen in the first line of the nation's favourite poem (see page 56).

Accents

Britain is full of diverse and distinctive accents. England, Wales, Scotland and Northern Ireland all boast their own individual dialect and pronunciation, while Welsh and Scottish Gaelic remain actively spoken and taught in schools.

Regional accents also abound, ranging from the 'Queen's English' to Yorkshire vernacular to the 'Scouse' Liverpudlian accent – and many more.

Cockney Rhyming Slang

One British dialect has even developed its own title: Cockney Rhyming Slang. Although typically associated with the East End of London, this rhyming style has spread all over the British Isles and continues to proliferate in modern times.

Rhyming slang describes a collection of phrases created from words that rhyme with any given word or expression. Here are some examples.

Apples and pears	Stairs
Dog and bone	Phone
Britney Spears	Beers
Pork pies	Lies
Raspberry tarts	Farts

'There are two seasons in Scotland. June and winter.'

Billy Connolly

The Bowler Hat

As far as British fashion goes, perhaps the most symbolic costume of the Briton is the bowler hat.

Originally seen as an informal alternative to the top hat, it was popularized by British Prime Minister Stanley Baldwin (1867–1947), as well as comedy icons Charlie Chaplin (1889–1977) and Laurel and Hardy.

'It was the nation and the race dwelling all round the globe that had the lion's heart. I had the luck to be called upon to give the roar.' Sir Winston Churchill

Sir James Dyson

(1947–)

O NE OF the most ingenious inventors of modern times, Norfolk-born Dyson's most famous creation is the 'bagless' vacuum cleaner, the design of which had previously remained largely unaltered since its launch in 1901.

After five years and 5,127 prototypes, Dyson perfected the G Force Dual Cyclone. Unable to gain a licence for the product in Europe, he took it to Japan, where it won the 1991 International Design Fair Prize.

Despite this, there was no interest from leading manufacturers, so Dyson set up his own factory in Wiltshire instead. He is now one of Britain's wealthiest men, credited with revolutionizing the domestic market.

The invention in fact came about by chance, when Dyson was working on another lucrative creation, the Ballbarrow: a wheelbarrow with a ball for a wheel.

Magna Carta

The most significant democratic document in history, this English charter, first issued by King John in 1215, established basic laws and human rights.

Some of its declarations remain part of Britain's laws today, including these two key clauses.

Clause 39

No free man shall be taken or imprisoned or dispossessed, or outlawed or exiled, or in any way destroyed, nor will we go upon him, nor will we send against him except by the lawful judgement of his peers or by the law of the land.

Clause 40

To no man will we sell, or deny, or delay, right or justice.

A Historic Document

Magna Carta has played a role in several historic moments.

For example, in England in the mid seventeenth century, it was cited in the struggle between Oliver Cromwell (1599–1658) and King Charles I (1600–1649).

In the eighteenth century, meanwhile, two of its clauses became part of the American Constitution in the Bill of Rights. Magna Carta inspired the Fifth and Sixth Amendments.

When the universal Declaration of Human Rights was presented to the United Nations in 1948, it was described as a 'Magna Carta for the future'.

Preserved For Our Times

Four copies of the original Magna Carta still exist. They are all held in England: two are in the British Library in London, a third is in Lincoln Cathedral, and the fourth is in Salisbury Cathedral.

THE GREATEST BRITON

In 2002, the BBC conducted a countrywide poll to find the greatest Briton of all time. Over a million people had their say in the survey.

This was the top ten.

1. Sir Winston Churchill
2. Isambard Kingdom Brunel
3. Diana, Princess of Wales
4. Charles Darwin
5. William Shakespeare
6. Sir Isaac Newton
7. John Lennon
8. Elizabeth I
9. Admiral Horatio Lord Nelson
10. Oliver Cromwell

Sir Winston Churchill

(1874–1965)

———————

Born at Blenheim Palace in Oxfordshire, Churchill's career began in the army. In 1900, he became a Conservative MP for Oldham, but later joined the Liberal party, holding several high posts in government over the following three decades.

When Neville Chamberlain (1869–1940) resigned as Prime Minister in May 1940, Churchill took his place. He refused to surrender to Nazi Germany, eventually leading Britain to victory in the Second World War in 1945.

Twice Prime Minister, he is one of the greatest politicians the world has ever known. An MP for over sixty-three years, he is also Britain's longest-serving parliamentarian.

Churchill simultaneously established an illustrious literary career, winning the Nobel Prize in Literature in 1953, the same year he was knighted. The first statesman to be granted a state funeral in the twentieth century,

Churchill is also remembered for his oratory skills and caustic wit.

> 'We shall not flag or fail. We shall go on to the end, we shall fight in France, we shall fight on the seas and oceans, we shall fight with growing confidence and growing strength in the air, we shall defend our Island, whatever the cost may be, we shall fight on the beaches, we shall fight on the landing grounds, we shall fight in the fields and in the streets, we shall fight in the hills; we shall never surrender.'
>
> Sir Winston Churchill, 4 June 1940

'To be born English is to have won first prize in the lottery of life.'

Cecil Rhodes